HR Means HERO: Handbook of A Marvelous Human Resource Specialist

Rachel Hays

Published by Rachel Hays, 2016.

HR MEANS HERO: HANDBOOK OF A MARVELOUS HUMAN RESOURCE SPECIALIST

First edition. September 9, 2016.

Written by Rachel Hays.

Introduction

"Not all heroes wear capes."

This is more than an internet meme. It's a fundamental truth for today's top-performing human resources professionals – the men and women who take an organization's most valuable resource and critically empower them to shape the future and define success. These men and women are HR Heroes because they seek to understand and support the most versatile, complex, nuanced and creatively powerful asset any organization has: its human employees.

Why are HR practitioners heroes? Consider all the losses which companies today shoulder because their best and brightest workers depart out of frustration and anger. Think of the influence HR Heroes wield when designing management systems that stop the outflow of talent and maximize the organization's people-power. Imagine being the prime factor in turning a company's sagging fortunes into a corporate powerhouse because its human workforce proudly showcases its achievements in the competitive marketplace.

Now picture yourself making that difference.

Whether you're charged with recruiting the company's future workforce, fine-tuning an enviable suite of employee benefits or offering comfort and support to an employee in crisis, HR Heroes are a critical element in an organization's ongoing strategic direction. Dive into the details here and see if you have the right stuff to be the sophisticated and highly-sought HR Hero for your choice of organization.

Having The Basics

What is Human Resources?

The resources of a company fall into many categories and come in different forms. Just as construction materials are used by builders to create homes, technology is utilized in the office to perform administration, and money funds the actions of the organization, these resources are all parts working in concert to drive the business engine. Employees are the human resources of an organization and are widely touted as the most important element of that corporate machine.

Simply put, successful Human Resource management means that given the right environment, tools, and rewards, employees can drive a company's competitive advantage.

Human Resource Functions

The breadth of Human Resource functions depends of a variety of factors ranging from organization size to the leadership's sense of value in this body of knowledge. In the interest of being comprehensive, Human Resource functions speak to activities performed in support of both employee and employer across the entire employment relationship:

Recruitment

Before we Human Resource Professionals can apply our knowledge of human motivational theories, emotional intelligence and learning styles, there must exist humans! In Human Resources, we will often handle the recruitment function which will involve:

Performing Job Analysis

The Maintenance Manager wants to hire a maintenance mechanic. "Sure, a maintenance mechanic!" you say! But wait, you don't work in maintenance! How do you hire the right person for a field that is so foreign to you?

You work in Human Resources. You went to school for Human Resources. You are not expected to know everything about every job out there; you are trained to know how to find out everything about every job out there.

So start finding out.

Ask the manager and members of the maintenance team what someone in this position would do in a typical day. Ask other maintenance mechanics what they have found to be the most important requirements for success in this role. Ask high performers what percentage of their time is spent doing different tasks. Ask recent hires if there are components to the role they didn't realize until coming on board (and include this in your notes). Ask the Maintenance Manager to explain his team's current weak points to identify skills most needed by the team.

Writing The Job Description

Does your organization already have job descriptions for each position? If so, does the current job description match the needs of the department today? Job descriptions can come in different shapes and sizes; the key is consistency.

How to Write a Job Description that Gets the Right Attention

'Help Wanted' and 'Now Hiring'- These are very common slogans used by employers around the world when posting job ads. These are also very bland slogans used by employers around the world when posting job ads! We live in a competitive labor market; to win the race for talent, employers must either know how to write a job description that gets attention from top candidates, or find someone who can.

Start with the Title

Would you rather be a Housekeeper or an Image Ambassador? Create titles that are unique; ones that draw attention, build interest, and give people pride in the work that they do. Just because other businesses in your industry advertise for Front Desk Clerks, nothing is stopping you from hiring a Welcome Team Member.

Working Environment

Does the position involve standing for long periods of time? Will the job require extensive travel? Be honest about the working conditions. Your new hire will eventually find out and you want that person to stay with your organization when they do!

Potential

Will you offer opportunities for professional or personal development? Does this position have advancement opportunities attached to it? These are the questions on job seekers' minds, and why should we wait until the interview to discuss these points?

Culture / Core Values

Use your job ad to educate candidates (and potential clientele, for that matter) on what makes your organization different from your competitors. There will be many candidates with skills matching the requirements of the role, but do their principles and priorities align with those of your organization?

The right people can give your department or company a competitive advantage. Write job descriptions that accurately describe the position and attract people who will fit well.

Determining The Right Sources for Talent

You have your job description. Even more, you feel a deep understanding of the position you are tasked with filling. Now it's time to start searching for that right person! But where?

If you perform an internet search for job posting sites, be assured you will find many more than are needed to fill this position. What's more, outside of the internet-based job sites, there are a range of other recruitment methods out there at your disposal.

Being a good recruiter is like being a good behavioral analyst – you need to think like the people you are trying to reach. Are you trying to find an IT specialist to run the rollout of your organization's new GIS? You may want to use some of those internet search sites. Are you looking for a seasoned transport driver for a regular Montana-to-Canada run? Highway billboards may work better here than an online ad.

A good recruiter is also an efficient recruiter. Always with the best interest of the business in mind, consider free or low cost, high-traffic options. Use word-of-mouth and consider employee referrals. Post job openings as the latest news within your organization on social media to increase your reach while saving the company recruitment costs.

Above all, keep abreast of your department's performance in drawing good hires. Over time, and with the help of simple spreadsheet tracking, you can determine trends where different professions tend to look for work; you can also track where your competitors are posting to ensure no opportunity to win talent is overlooked.

Reviewing & Screening Candidates

You are visited by a supervisor who needs to hire for a big upcoming project. She says "I just need a body" but as a HERO in HR you know that simply filling a position does not a successful fill make. We want to find the best person for the job so once applications start to come in, it helps to have screening parameters. For instance, if this is an entry-level labor position that involves driving, you might want to make driver history a key part in assessing candidates. A candidate with great experience but recent incidents of reckless driving and failures to obey traffic regulations may not be the person you want operating your company vehicles.

Providing a Realistic Job Preview

Always the business partner, the HR HERO can decrease turnover due to poor fit by presenting a fuller picture of the position early in the screening process. A realistic job preview might consist of a video of the job, interviews with current employees discussing pros and cons they experience in the role, or a simulation experience where candidates are exposed to an actual day in the role.

A potential Indoor Food Sampler might love to find out that you get to taste-test your samples – yum! However, spending that trial day standing in one spot for 8 hours is harder than expected. In this way, your applicant is able to weigh elements of the job that cannot be experienced in simply reading the posting.

Have a senior employee take potential candidates for a walking tour of the entire mill – all 2 acres – dressed in heavy PPE, meeting the teams, climbing a few stories to different work areas, stopping by the full service cafeteria for a quick coffee all while taking in the dust, noise and occasional monotony of the plant. One candidate might feel a great fit with the people but cannot stand to be inside a building lacking windows for 12 hours a day. Another potential employee may return with a coffee and a smile, having always worked in noisy, dusty environments and impressed with the size of the building.

RJPs can be implemented in different ways for different roles, but the aim is to avoid investing the time and money in hiring and training people only to have them quit because they do not actually like the job.

Interviewing for Success

The Interview. In most workplaces, the interview is the final showdown; the Make It or Break It, Sink-or-Swim, Face-to-Face meeting between you and potential new team members. You need to ask the right questions to hire the right person. Hold meaningful interviews; ask questions that require more from the interviewee than the standard queries anyone can search for (and thus prepare for) online. Ask your candidate questions that highlight the person behind the resume to establish their fit with your organization.

Good Questions to Ask in an Interview as an Employer

"Tell us a little about yourself."

Beginning with an open-ended and seemingly unrelated question like this builds rapport with your candidate and allows them time to freely talk and acclimate to the interview environment. Their level of comfort will often determine your ability to see their true personality.

"If you were hiring someone for this position, what would you look for?"

This is not a common interview question. When a candidate is asked a question they are not expecting, their answers tend to be less rehearsed and more candid. How well does the candidate understand the role or the business in general? Their answer here will tell you.

"Describe the things that frustrate you and how you deal with them?"

Conflict is not a bad word but it is inevitable in life and certainly in the workplace. Answers to this question will give insight on how your candidate views and approaches conflict, frustrations and problems. With this, you can decide if their viewpoint and approach matches the values of your organization.

"What are 3 positive things you last boss would say about you?"

Don't ask candidates to list their strengths and weaknesses. They expect this question and they have prepared for it. Catch them off guard and ask them instead what others would say their strengths and weaknesses are. The answers may be quite different. Following an interview, a seasoned recruiter might conduct reference calls with that last boss to compare.

"What role do you usually take in a team setting?"

Your entire establishment is a team. This question can help you to anticipate how a potential candidate will contribute to their immediate team and to your business in general. This question can elicit a variety of information for you to consider; their answer may speak to their motivation or their personality. It may shine light on a candidate's level of autonomy or potential for moving up in the future.

"Do you have any questions for us?"

Best. Question. Ever. Although this is a pretty standard question, reversing roles communicates that the company seeks an open dialogue, and it helps you to ascertain just how curious and knowledgeable a candidate is about your company. If s/he doesn't ask any questions about the job or the business, it's a safe bet her/his heart isn't in it.

As an employer, you understand the interview session is an integral part of the recruitment process. Remember to make the interview count and ask good questions.

Selection

In working with the department manager to analyze the position, you will have developed a good understanding of what kind of hire they need but the final decision is typically made with, if not solely by, the manager.

As HR professionals, honor the relationship you have made on behalf of the organization with all candidates contacted during the selection stage of the recruitment process. If they impressed you enough to get to the interview stage, but were not the best fit for the current position, maintain that link in case they might be the star for a future role.

If you are asked to explain your decision not to hire a candidate, be honest with your feedback. Tell the job seeker that showing up to the interview twenty-five minutes late, combined with long delays in their returning follow up calls, caused the hiring team to question their reliability. Going forward, that candidate might view timeliness as a greater priority, which will benefit them in any future job.

Orientation & Onboarding

In this profession, the HR department oversees the orientation – largely the administration – of new hires. You will add them to employee rosters and contact lists, guide them through payroll and benefits setup, and answer or direct any questions along the way. Alternatively, you may become part of a company that prefers onboarding to orientation.

No matter, in Human Resources we try to impact employees at every turn (for the better, of course!). Outside of the regular paperwork, consider including these elements to your new hire program:

Introducing the Company, the Department and the Team

Does your company have an organizational chart? And if so, how detailed is it? Some organizational charts simply show the executive level appointments while others lay out each department with the appropriate communication or reporting channels of each. Whatever the format, it is a great idea to start a new employee off at the org chart like a traveler starts his journey with a map.

Housekeeping items are so often forgotten – where are the washrooms, change rooms, first aid and muster stations? Is there a code to dial out? Is there a code to enter the building? Make sure the work station, tools and materials needed for your new hire to start work are set up and organized for their first day so they aren't left sitting in reception, wondering if anyone was anticipating their arrival.

Identify a buddy, trainer or team resource for your new hire who is a great performer and teammate – nothing worse than training with someone who is uncomfortable or unsure!

Delivering an Employee Handbook

In addition to the hire package – pay, benefits and tax forms - the employee handbook is one of the first and most important documents an employee can have, typically containing policies and procedures regarding different aspects of an employee's life within the company, such as the following:

- Privacy of Information (both the employee's and the employer's)

- Code of Conduct which outlines ethical and professional standards within and outside the workplace

- Harassment and Workplace Violence policies

- Drug and Alcohol policies

- Vacation and other pay policies

- Computer, Social Media and Cell Phone Usage standards of practice.

It is important, when building or reviewing the employee handbook, to look at the industry standards and consult with the leadership team to gain feedback on what works, what doesn't fit, and what's missing. A great practice is to perform an annual policy review, sharing any changes or additions with employees and explaining them in detail.

A handbook or policy cannot possibly account for everything that could happen in the workplace. Many situations have to be addressed on their own merit and so there is typically a caveat that a manager retains the right to manage – to use their own discretion with regard to policy application. For the most part, though, the employee handbook provides a ueful resource for employees as a first place to look for answers.

Developing the Training Plan

Even when welcoming an experienced hire, a training plan will be necessary. The work performed will likely be very similar to what the employee has performed in the past, but the environment, team, and organizational culture are new. Consult senior team members, department leadership and safety personnel to compile the competencies necessary for success in this role.

The resulting blueprint will contain proficiencies with an expected training time of 1 week; Others may tend to take up to 3 months. A great training plan allows for a sign-off by both trainer and trainee to indicate when they feel training has been sufficient. A copy is kept by both and once completed to the team's satisfaction, the training plan is placed in the employee's file to demonstrate this progress.

Following Up

In Human Resources there are many responsibilities that can keep us at our desks, but as a promoter of the organization as an employer of choice, it is important to get in front of the employee group as often as possible while cultivating relationships and "checking the pulse" of the people.

This goes double for new people. They may have lots of questions and often do not know who to ask for help. Reaching out to them will give them that inspiration to ask, and finding those answers will improve their initial experience.

Consider holding a follow-up day for new hires where they can come back to Human Resources and provide feedback to the organization on missing items identified during their initial employment period. This information can help fine-tune orientation and onboarding programs throughout the organization.

Performance Management

While you have interviewed for success - choosing candidates who emulate the desirable characteristics found in your finest employees - this doesn't mean those hires will succeed on their own.

Enter the art of performance management, where we mold character into actions with measurable results.

Performance Reviews

A job description should match its corresponding performance review. In fact, part of any performance review would require assessment and discussion around the employee's job description (with newer employees this would also include their training plan to mark progress). Some organizations tie pay to performance reviews so this requires total clarity prior to the meeting.

Performance reviews will vary according to the needs of the organization and the position. A member of the executive team might have annual strategies tied to business plans that will be reviewed as key performance indicators, whereas a finishing line operator's performance review may be based on the output of all members of the team.

Determining the Performance Review Team

Having a Human Resources professional in the performance meeting allows for a mediator to provide an outside opinion or objective guidance at points of disagreement. The HR practitioner should be available to both employee and manager following the performance meeting, connecting the employee with training and career path information, offering consultation on performance plans, and providing copies of documentation as appropriate and requested.

Obviously, the employee's supervisor should be present, if not presenting the review. Other members of leadership or a union representative beside the employee may also be invited to attend.

Delivering a Performance Review

It is important that the performance review never contain information that would come as a surprise to the employee. Employees should come into the performance review having a good idea of what to expect – understanding how they have been performing against goals, quotas, standards, etc. and understanding what their areas for improvement are. This mutual understanding should be fostered throughout the performance period with feedback, coaching and counselling. Manager notes should reflect the communication that has already taken place between employee and manager to date.

If a performance review does come as a shock to the employee, take time to consider communication with the employee up to this point. Likely, opportunities have been missed for development or acknowledgement. Identify where communication has lapsed and offer to help develop better strategies to ensure future feedback on performance occurs consistently.

Outside the Performance Review

The performance review should be an opportunity to delve into issues already identified. Both parties should arrive prepared to develop plans for improvement or movement onto new opportunities. Discussions around projects, responsibilities, and career paths are all likely to happen; use the mighty agenda to keep the conversation on topic!

Employee Relations

Your employer has employees and those employees will have relations - or interactions - within the company. In Human Resources, you will be asked to provide guidance to both employees and managers on how to handle certain relations. The circumstances can vary greatly around employee relations so many considerations come into play here.

External Legislation and Best Practice

Always consult the external legislation applicable to the situation, be it human rights statutes, employment law or contract law. Even a seasoned HR professional will review the applicable legislation before advising on employee relations, as legislation and court precedents change over time and we need to ensure compliance. Be mindful of the industry's best practices and incorporate these into your organization.

Remember that taking time to research before advising managers on appropriate steps is not an indication of incompetence or lack of knowledge in your field. It actually signals the opposite – a marvelous HR specialist takes time to consider all the facts and compare them with the available body of knowledge and legislation to ensure an accurate and up-to-date response.

Internal HR policies

Next, your internal policies – namely your HR Standards of Practice – will be a guide that must not conflict with the external legislation. Rather, it should complement the legislative environment with details of actions and considerations in various situations. Following both external legislation and internal SOPs lays a foundation of consistency and fairness for employee relations, eliminating areas where personal opinions or emotional responses can come into play.

Incident Investigations

When allegations arise involving employees in the organization, HR will carry out investigations, produce findings and provide guidance on actionable items. No matter the incident – a physical altercation among team mates, a complaint of sexual harassment by a supervisor, a reported safety infraction – some principles apply universally to investigations.

- Documentation – Document conversations with anyone involved; document findings and proof discovered in investigations; document the actions that arise from investigations. Documentation provides a history of the event and the grounds on which any decisions are made, in case an audit or dispute arises.

- Confidentiality – Investigations involve private information that is not to be shared with the rest of the organization, in the company newsletter, or at the dinner table that evening. HR professionals have a duty to protect the information they handle, keeping documentation in a secure location and understanding the rules of disclosure around the information they keep.

Mediation

HR Specialists often step in as mediators in conflict. While most would cringe at the word conflict, you know that conflict is not a bad word! Interpersonal tensions are inevitable as we all bring different backgrounds, viewpoints and personalities to the workplace. A successful enterprise actually needs diverse opinions and perspectives to make it well rounded and productive!

If you are heading into mediation, negotiations or another form of communication event, prepare participants with these rules of engagement to set the framework for a positive event:

Mind your Manners!

A less-than-desirable meeting (or meeting partner) will not be improved with disrespect. Instead, require all participants to maintain good manners or run the risk of ineffective communication and, therefore, an ineffective meeting. (And there is nothing worse than wasted time in a busy work day).

Good manners set a good platform for the meeting. Being punctual lets others know that you care about this conversation; being late reeks of disregard and impertinence. A gracious greeting and a handshake makes people feel welcomed and demonstrates openness and approachability to the present agenda. Imagine, instead, walking into that same setting and failing to acknowledge or greet your communication partners. Your colleagues will likely feel uncomfortable and on edge; certainly not the way to start a productive session. Small acts can make a big difference.

Emotions, Check!

In any communication setting, we are bound to have emotions that threaten to surface. Conflict situations involve opposing viewpoints, which can evoke tension, animosity and other intense sentiments. Maybe the topic raised touches you personally or evokes sad, painful memories. Perhaps the person(s) you are meeting with has upset you with their tone or words. An internal reaction is to be expected, but steer clear of an external display of what's happening inside.

Raising your voice, lashing out with words, or showing a menacing expression may be what you want to do; but remember that just because you may feel you have a right to do something, that doesn't make it the right thing to do. Heightened emotions can muddy the waters, preventing you from acting out of business sense. Your display may, in turn, induce emotions from your colleagues, and round and around we go, on a roller coaster ride without destination and certainly without results.

The Art of Active Listening

When people communicate, they have two goals in mind; to have their words acknowledged and to have you agree with said words. One of the greatest lessons in communication is that we can break down walls and create a satisfying experience for both parties; while you cannot always agree, you can always give acknowledgement to your communication partner. Enter active listening to your arsenal of communication barrier bombs!

Active listening is the practice of focusing on what your counterpart is saying. Sounds easy enough, right? Ask yourself, have you ever 'listened' to a colleague speaking, while forming your rebuttal in your head? You may feel like you are hearing everything the other person in saying, but this lack of focus is preventing you from gaining the complete message. Reject distracting thoughts, avoid interrupting and resist forming opinions and responses. A good test – and the appropriate response – to show you have been actively listening is to provide feedback to your partner. Repeat what you have heard in their message. This not only acknowledges what they are trying to communicate, but will provide opportunity for them to clarify if your comprehension does not match their intended message.

Body Language

Body language is a type of nonverbal communication that we bring with us into communication events, often without even noticing it ourselves. While you may be oblivious to your body language, your audience is certainly aware of the unspoken messages you are sending them. Be mindful of this as you enter your meeting space and work through issues.

What do you want your nonverbal messages to say? If you want to say 'I am engaged in this session', nod or smile at regular intervals to show them you are listening. Sit up straight and keep your hands on your laps or the arm rests to avoid appearing unfocused or distracted. Maintain a polite, appropriate degree of eye contact and a calm disposition to indicate an open mind.

Organization is Key

Do not fear the paperclip, the sticky note, or the highlighter! They are friends to communication, in that they can help you ensure that your agenda and item points are clear and concise.

Organization really is the key to successful communication because a warm welcome and proper eye contact will not get your agenda to your communication partners. Ensure your points are written, itemized and arranged, perhaps in order of importance or deadline. You should be prepared to introduce each item, explain their background or business case and articulate their merit. Also, try to anticipate the questions and/or concerns that may be raised and prepare your responses ahead of time. Bring your laptop and take notes if this helps you to take away learnings from the session.

Disciplinary Actions

Have you coached and counselled the employee you are about to discipline, or does the act merit immediate disciplinary action? These are questions HR may ask managers seeking guidance or assistance in composing a written warning or conducting a disciplinary meeting. In Human Resources, we want to make sure the event is documented appropriately.

No one likes to be disciplined at work. It can be uncomfortable, embarrassing and stressful. However, discipline may become necessary for employees who break the rules or continually underperform. Disciplinary actions can be communicated with the aim of impressing upon employees both the significance of this event and their importance to the team. From a business standpoint, it can be more efficient – in terms of time and finances - to work with a current employee on a performance issue than to replace them. From a human standpoint, salvaging a wayward employee is a skill and a success for the team which communicates that employees are highly valued to the organization. Such successes will reap future rewards many times over.

Termination

It is possible to terminate someone on a good note! As an HR professional, one of your greatest skills is your ability to find opportunity in failure, motivating people even when they must be dismissed from your team. This can only be accomplished with honesty.

There is a huge difference between terminating on a good note and sugarcoating a dismissal. Give people the gift of feedback. If an employee was regularly late for work, don't shy away from explaining this as the reason they are being let go. Tell them that their lateness has impacted their team's performance and implied an attitude of nonchalance to their work and the company. This gives them the opportunity to improve for with their next employer.

Communication and Engagement

Communication is a prime area of opportunity for employers to improve. While we cannot always disclose every detail of executive decisions or provide notice of company changes until they are decided, HR professionals are often given the authority to develop communication practices that strengthen company bonds across levels or locations of the operation.

Communications Strategy

A communications strategy is a great time investment; there should be rules around communication do's and don'ts of your teams. A communications strategy will outline the company's regular communication practices, such as a monthly newsletter, annual town halls, employee suggestion boxes, and quarterly memos from the President on the company's outlook.

A communications strategy might also outline appropriate modes communication at your workplace, such as advising that email is not considered an appropriate means to discuss conflict-prone matters.

Does your organization want to regulate the subject matter of communications during company time or using company resources? Consider advising staff that profanity in communications will be a matter of discipline. A social media and internet usage policy many also be included here, providing notice to employees that the organization has the ability and authority to monitor employee usage of company electronics. Remind your employees that a public embarrassment ignited by poor conduct on social media can harm everyone's reputation and put the company in serious risk.

Finding the Right Communications for your Organization

Communication is not a "one size fits all" business application. While your administrative staff likely have continual access to email messages at their work stations, your field technicians won't and may even find themselves out of the service area to even receive messages on their mobile phones.

When choosing or advising on the right communication modes for your organization, you need to consider more than the environment and demographics of your workforce. Consider the type of information being communicated. Corporate decisions affecting the entire organization such as a merger, closure or acquisition are best communicated in person, through the executive, and with allotted time or resources for questions and concerns. Daily safety meetings might be better held at a departmental level if work groups are spread across different locations. Besides, the location and activity of each department will affect the priorities for each team.

Employee Engagement

It is said that a good leader can motivate others to work harder for him or her than they would for themselves. For an HR professional who wants to move beyond the administration of people, employee engagement is about creating the right conditions and environment to change satisfaction to passion, employment to commitment, and work to effort. Consider the following in employee motivation here:

Motivational Programs

The staple of a successful motivational program is that it must not become a staple! Motivational programs must be ever changing, to keep employees engaged and encouraged by the program.

Find or build programs that incentivize performance in areas where improvement is needed, not areas where things are already working well.

Also, run programs that are based on objective criteria, not subjective selection, otherwise the program will lose its credibility fast!

And remember: people respond to incentives. Be sure you reward the actual behavior you want and don't get caught in a mess of unintended outcomes.

Rewards

What counts as a reward to you, may not count as a reward to the next guy! Take an organization that brings its top performers – Housekeeper of the Year, Maintenance Person of the Year, Customer Service Representative of the Year, you get the drift – on a trip to Las Vegas! Sounds great! But wait, now your top housekeeper – making $13/hour - has to not only take time off (unpaid or with vacation time) for this trip, but she can't afford to take in any of the shows or entertainment available along the strip. Sounds more stressful than anything. That housekeeper might prefer the monetary value of the trip to pay for back-to-school clothes or an extracurricular activity for her children instead. So then, we must consider the demographics, needs and wants of our employee group when making sure our rewards are actually rewarding for them.

In addition to monetary or material rewards, the gift of acknowledgement goes a long way! "Employee Of The Month" parking spots, kudos at the safety meeting or a pat on the back in the company newsletter make employees feel valuable. As in the case of fringe benefits, use the opportunities already available that you may be overlooking.

Employee Engagement Surveys and Results

A great survey is one where employees are given ample time to complete as opposed to a manager pushing to simply have a 100% response rate for corporate reporting.

A great survey asks questions that are open-ended, allowing employees the opportunity to voice ideas and concerns in greater detail that a 5-point rating system sometimes allows. (This said, rating systems are common because they're simpler to design and tabulate, making them very efficient. They do serve a purpose and cannot be entirely discounted).

Whatever the format, leadership must consider and apply the feedback received. Now, it would be impractical to expect an employer to implement a solution to every concern or area of opportunity overnight. As a leadership group, select opportunities that can be worked on and regularly go back to the employee group with action-item progress reports. Feedback in motion will increase employee engagement and employee survey participation.

Employees as Employer Ambassadors

Employees are our best advertising medium. If we are an employer of choice, employees will tell everyone they know; they will refer friends and tell others about the great team they have and the acknowledgement they receive. This is more effective than any other online advertisement could be. Alternatively, ignore employees or prevent them from having a voice in the company, and they will also tell everyone they know.

One great way of making an employee an ambassador is highlighting them, maybe on your website or on a job posting. Have them explain in words or a short video clip what they would tell future employees or potential stakeholders about the organization.

Compensation and Benefits

The younger generations entering today's job market are seeking work-life balance, job satisfaction, motivational programs and a host of other feel-good toppings on the cake. But young or old, workers work to provide the lives they seek for themselves and their families. Compensation and benefits is one area where HR professionals are able to show direct impact to budget to the C-Suite and extrinsically attract and retain individuals.

Compensation Policies

Compensation policies may be included with human resource policies in the employee handbook or a similar document. Such policies might include:

- Timekeeping – How is the employee or manager involved in the timekeeping process and what are the associated deadlines?

- Overtime Rules – Does the employee require manager approval to work overtime? How are overtime hours claimed?

- Banked Time Agreements – Do they apply to all employees?

- Vacation Policies – Does your organization credit vacation into the employee's account at the beginning of every year or is vacation time accrued?

- How is the employee or manager involved in the timekeeping process and what are the deadlines associated?

Oftentimes, even with the payroll department right next door, the HR office is where people will visit to ask such questions so it's important that Human Resources and Payroll are very connected in any well-run organization. Payroll may even report into the HR department within the organizational chart.

Benefit Programs

HR will be a key figure in choosing benefit programs that satisfy both the majority of employee group needs and the budgetary parameters of the employer. It is important to look at each offering of the benefit plan in your workplace and investigate its utilization rate among your employee group. Is there a preference for a larger Health Spending Account and less specific Paramedical Benefits? Do employees want a short-term disability program just as much as a long-term disability program? It is a good practice to review and consider a number of providers and ensure you understand the fine print of each contract.

Fringe Benefits

What are the perks that matter to your employees? Childcare? Parking? Gym memberships? Again, the demographics of your workforce will determine what fits for the majority of the group. There are organizations that connect their employees with a personal assistant services which help with anything in their life outside work, from grocery shopping to grabbing that must-have coffee. Some companies that make use of options already present in the business. For example, a hotel management company might offer discounted room rates or use of the pool for employees and their families – this is at little cost to the organization and requires even less administration.

Total Compensation

Compensation – like communication – is another area where employees always seem to be left wanting more (go figure!). An annual Total Compensation Report is a great tool for employers to show employees the "hidden money" they make. Together, Human Resources and Payroll can provide an annual statement to employees that might include:

- Base pay

- Bonuses, including any one-time bonuses for that year

- Monetary value of vacation, sick days, and any other paid leave

- Employer's financial contribution to health, dental, vision, life, and short/long-term disability insurance

- Employer's financial contribution to the employee's retirement plan, such as a 401(k) or pension plan

- Stock options

- Employer's financial contribution to the Employee Assistance Program (on a per-employee basis)

- Vehicle or cell phone allowances

- Fitness club memberships (or the value of the discount attained through the employer)

- On-site child care

- Free or discounted public transportation or parking

- Tuition assistance or relocation expenses

Include here even those perks that do not have a monetary value, so that the total compensation statement shows the whole picture. This might include benefits like flex time or on-site facilities available for employee use.

This tool can make the difference in employee morale, performance and retention. In this way, base pay is no long the only variable considered when comparing other job offers.

Health and Wellness

While we may support or handle health and safety programs in the workplace, HR professionals are always central to employee Health and Wellness programs.

Health and Wellness Programs

With people working until later in life and the greater body of knowledge and emphasis placed on health and work-life balance, employers are getting more involved with supportive initiatives. The only limitation when it comes to Health and Wellness initiatives is your imagination. Local hospitals and gyms may offer ready-made options that appeal to your teams. Alternatively, you may decide to develop a program. There is a galaxy of websites where you can get great ideas and resources to help inspire.

Employee Assistance Programs

Employee Assistance Plans are a common component of employee fringe benefits, typically providing free and anonymous counselling services for employees and their family members on topics such as financial planning, marriage and family conflict, health and wellness assessments and legal advice. This is a very valuable but often overlooked resource for employees, so understanding the parameters of the program and regularly reminding the team will ensure better usage. If you are the HR professional responsible for choosing your organization's EAP, do take your time and consider the following:

- Cost of the program and options around a significant increase or decrease in employee numbers

- Parameters of each service offered, such as number of free counselling sessions available
- Applicability of the program (if your workplace runs 24 hours a day / 7 days a week, you may need support programs that do the same or create a team of in-house peer advisors to bridge immediate needs with extended care provided by the EAP outside of work).

Crisis Management

As an HR professional, you are likely to experience some of the best and worst moments of an employee's life with them and with their families. While we cannot plan for every possible emergency, employees and leaders benefit from regular training in their responsibilities given such circumstances. Should that situation arise, you will have more people who understand what to do and not as many people who need to be guided. Should a situation arise outside of your training, your teams will have a place to start and understand the process of developing an appropriate plan and assigned responsibilities.

What is your place when a crisis situation arises? Members of leadership and the safety team are working on the incident investigation, while Public Relations and the executive are handling the media. Your role is clear. In Human Resources, our number one priority is our company's humans. In a crisis, there will likely be employees on location and employees not on location. Personal contact with each member of the team is not always a possibility, but some form of contact should take place with everyone. Be on-side during employee debriefings to provide empathy, a listening ear and a connection with additional supports needed.

Information Management

Documentation resulting from hiring, policy acknowledgements, training, health and safety, pay and benefits and performance management can amount to a small mountain of paper. How do we best organize, record, track and retain this information?

Employee Files

There are as many ways to organize employee files as there are employee files to organize! This may seem daunting – indeed, filing is a tedious task – but is also a necessary labor. This is the first place you will go to find an employee's emergency contact information in the event of an emergency; it is where a new manager will find the performance history on each of his new direct reports.

How do we best organize it all? This will typically depend on your preference. For instance, a different color folder for safety documents, training certificates and payroll information could certainly create ease in locating information in a hurry.

How do we keep information up-to-date? Going forward from initial setup, regular audits of employee files will help ensure documentation is current (ensure employees regularly confirm their address and emergency contacts for example).

Human Resource Information Management System

Ah, HRIMS (the Human Resource Information Management System) - an HR professional's dream; the answer to eliminating rooms filled with file cabinets and mountains of paper. An HRIMS can provide time efficiencies by eliminating the need to manually search and pull information from files. An HRIMS can manage performance review and training tracking of employees, allowing it to compile succession plans and career path progress reports on employees. Adding to efficiency, the HRIMS allows employees to own part of the information management process through Employee Service sections, where workers can update their contact information, performance and record goal-setting and request vacation or other payroll functions.

Record Retention Regulations

How long must resumes vs. payroll records be kept? Can terminated employees request access to their employee files? Consult local, state and federal legislation regarding record retention; the applicable laws will differ depending on the document and the company's location, so protect your organization and make sure your practices are compliant.

Engage Your Supports

Understanding the Industry

We have reviewed the basics of Human Resources, but understanding which functions to employ in your HR department, and how best to roll out new initiatives, will largely depend on your industry. An oilfield company enjoying a high in the market would be focused on recruitment. With lots of new hires, they might also be very concerned about proper orientation or onboarding. A hotel management company planning a 6 property acquisition may need an HR person or team providing input and guidance on communication strategy and change management.

Human Resources is a profession that will allow you to work in any type of workplace. In this way, HR requires a dual specialization; understanding human relations, and understanding the industry in which these human relations take place. Talk to employees at every level and in every department and work to understand how each relate to the other. Shadow the work being done and understand the organization's goals, marketplace and competitors. This insight will support your decisions and actions and give you credibility among employees.

Network

To do this, we need to leave our office, and indeed, the doors of the organization!

Volunteer

Volunteer with your certification board to be a mentor to emerging HR professionals – this will likely offer a mutual learning experience as your mentee is fresh out of school and well-versed on the newest trends - or join the association's chapter committee to help spearhead local professional development events. You will meet other HR professionals and other leaders who have valuable experiences to share.

Join the Local Professional Community

Does your city have a chamber of commerce which hosts regular social events to encourage networking among local businesses and professionals? If not, the city likely offers committee or board positions; why not get involved in initiatives directly impacting your organization or profession?

Other Resources

https://www.shrm.org/

The Society for Human Resource Management (SHRM) has 285,000 members from more than 165 countries. Joining this society means being connected with a leading provider of resources serving the needs of HR professionals and advancing the practice of human resource management.

http://www.hrmamerica.com/

HRM America offers readers high-quality, timely and informative news on the HR profession, as well as insightful opinions and best-practices articles from some of the brightest minds in HR and people management.

http://humancapitalmedia.com/

Human Capital Media (HCM) is a media resource covering topics, events and research findings on human capital, management and workforce development.

Additionally, check out Linked:HR - the top Human Resources Group on LinkedIn with over a half million members and hundreds of active discussions monthly. Human Resources Professionals Worldwide is the second most popular group to connect you with discussions and professions relative to your practice.

Reaching Senior Leadership

Business Acumen

Being a member of the executive means determining strategic direction of the business. Consider the following:

Alignment with Organizational Strategy

A great HR Specialist aligns department actions with the organization's strategic direction. If the company is looking at cost-cutting due to market pressures, it is probably not the best time to present a possible HRIMS to the leadership. Continue with the manual files for the time being as an HRMIS is an elective cost. If the organization seeks to gain competitive advantage in terms of its customer service, your department might bring forward training sessions in communication skills for handling difficult customers.

The field of Human Resources offers an exciting array of options to implement in the workplace, but we must make sure that the initiative satisfies the needs of the organization, not just our love for practicing HR!

Anticipating Needs

As an Executive Human Resource Leader, you will determine policy and initiatives for the organization. Make sure you deliver proactive initiatives instead of reactive solutions.

Keep in touch with other department leaders to understand upcoming operational projects, changes, and challenges. Visit regularly with local economic development officers in your areas of operation to understand the economy and marketplace of the industry. Keep a keen eye on trends in Human Resource practice, and in your employer's industry, to understand new opportunities.

Presentation Vs. Presence

As a member of the executive, you will need to be able to present. You could be called upon to give quarterly departmental updates to the owner group or speak on behalf of the organization regarding new employee initiatives. In either case, companies want leaders who can draw out the passion of its workforce. You need to reach beyond your PowerPoint slides to engage your audience and secure buy-in.

Representing the employer and answering the tough questions in front of an audience is not for the fainthearted or ill-prepared. This requires a speaker who is confident, sharp and personable. Luckily, public speaking is a skill that can be learned.

You can find a selection of self-help literature with tools and tips on how to prepare for different speaking engagements or improve your staging. Alternatively, seek out the support of your local Toastmasters group, an assembly of individuals who practice public speaking with one another to strengthen their skills and comfort level.

Demonstrating Return On Investment

Human Resources is often viewed as an administrative function; an overhead cost of running an organization. A savvy HR professional is able to change this viewpoint, demonstrating that we can impact a company's bottom line just like operations or purchasing. Consider the following examples:

- By using your recruitment functions to hire employees with industry experience and a history of safe work practices, your organization sees a decrease in new-hire safety incidents coupled with savings on disability, replacement and legal costs.
- By providing realistic job previews and conducting pre-employment activities that accurately prepare candidates for their prospective employment, you lower first-year turnover.

- By hiring locally instead of relocating and hiring candidates with the required industry certifications (instead of paying for training upon hire), you bring in employees who can hit the ground running at a lower cost.
- By working on communication and employee engagement to create a happy and healthy team, you can report decreased absenteeism and increased productivity.

This is bona-fide Return on Investment. Now, you are not an overhead cost, but a business partner who contributes to the company's success. All of these measures can and should be tracked. Showcasing the monetary value of our actions and programs gains buy-in for future initiatives and credibility in the department's – and your own - value to the organization.

Employer Branding

Your organization has a service or product that it brands to customers and clients. Likewise, your organization has to advertise to its internal customers – its employees or potential employees – as an employer of choice. Enter "employer branding", where your organization decides what message it wants people to hear when considering a spot on the team. You must ask your leadership and your employees: what best describes your organization, what are the reasons your current employees chose to come on board and, moreover, to stay on board? Is this the message you want to represent the organization? If not, determine what your ideal message is and put steps in place to achieve it before promoting it.

Determining Your Core Values

What types of behaviors and events get rewarded and celebrated within your organization? Perhaps you find that you have a Sales Leader of the Month program but you do not announce or celebrate birthdays or work anniversaries. This would indicate that sales performance might be a core value whereas employees' personal events are not – this may not be improper but it should be understood.

To determine your organization's core values, consider inviting a diverse group of employees and managers to come together, learn about what core values are and hold focus groups. Gather input on what your workforce has experienced as the company's core values.

Decisions made based on the organization's core values lends them substance and can make decision making easier. Connecting company actions or events to core values will start to build an entire employee group that identifies with and aligns their work efforts to these values.

Policy Development

As HR Leaders, we are often called upon to provide guidance or mediation on employment matters. While some issues are governed by legislation external to our workplace, many employers seek to address the leftover grey areas with internal policies and procedures. So, then, it makes sense that internal human resource policies be written by human resource professionals.

Creating a Standard of Practice

Any internal legislation should not conflict with (nor can it override) external legislation governing the same issue. Internal legislation is meant to add to external legislation. For instance, the minimum wage is set externally for all industries, however, an employer has the right to hire employees at a rate exceeding the minimum wage; they just cannot hire at a rate less than the minimum wage.

Additionally, a standard of practice should be reasonable. It would be impractical to have internal legislation requiring weekly performance reviews for a group of 50 executives. There simply would not be enough time to allow for follow-through, leading to a breakdown in policy versus practice and undermining policy credibility. Instead, creating a standard of having quarterly goal reviews between executive and manager to review progress and assess the project with weekly action item updates could be practical.

Supervisor Standards Of Practice Training

Standards require leadership support from the top or they simply will not be adopted as standards. And leaders cannot be expected to practice policies and procedures of which they are unaware! Thus, new leaders (managers, supervisors, etc.) should partake in Standards of Practice (SOP) training. This is best done in a group setting with a number of new leaders so that great discussion can take place and questions get asked that some participant may not have considered.

Leaders should not be expected to memorize the standards of practice, just as employees are not expected to memorize their handbook. The intention of training is to provide leaders with an idea of the SOP scope so they will be mindful of SOPs when pertinent events arise.

Regular Policy Reviews

Annual policy reviews should take place against external legislation to ensure policies are still compliant with the related laws. Similarly, internal practices should be audited to identify those which are unsuccessful. Leader must have input here to ensure standards match the needs of the organization.

Owning Your Industry

Human Resource Education

While some HR skills are inherent – you either have the ability to empathize with the struggles of others, or you don't – other skills are taught; and while some professionals enter the field through internal movement within their organization, most employers desire a formal education in their HR practitioners.

Job Shadowing

When considering any career, it is a great idea to look for opportunities to job-shadow; Human Resources is no exception. Reading about a profession will provide you with general career path information; seeing it in action may help you decide on whether you wish to travel that path!

Additionally, keep in mind that Human Resources is a practice which is employed in virtually every industry out there – so in addition to feeling out the field of Human Resources, it is good to also consider your potential industry of practice. Would you prefer a jeans and workboot plant, supporting a shiftwork environment? Perhaps a corporate setting involving travel to different office locations is more preferable. Think seriously about the physical work environment and schedule, the dress code, travel requirements/opportunities, and the functional components of the work.

Diplomas, Certificates, and Degrees!

There are a ton of great websites that can connect the career with the school - they are easy to use and have extra resources that can provide tuition calculators, format choices and skills assessments. Some organizations allow for training expenses, supporting their employees to return to school and complete programming to receive their official certification

Certification Boards

Find out if there is a local, state or national certification board. This extra certification may require proof of professional experience, an interview, testing and a small fee for membership; however, the benefits can be significant. Certification shows an alignment of your practice with the standards of excellence in your field and your membership will help keep you connected with other HR professionals. You'll discover new trends emerging in the industry and potential opportunities for employment.

Human Resource Skillset

As in any profession, there are levels of practice within Human Resources but there remain some key skills sought in the character of an HR practitioner at all levels.

Confidentiality

In an advisory role, you will conduct investigations and advise on employee relations. At an administrative level, you will handle an employee's most personal information – their address, banking, health and family information – and control access to this information. As an executive, you will likely take part in discussions around financials and major company changes.

No matter the title, the content you work with will require discretion. You must be able to retain and manage information according to standards of privacy legislation and organizational protocol.

Ability to Navigate the Grey

Working in human resources, you will work with the guidelines of multiple external legislative bodies as well as internal policy. You will encounter situations where all of the above come into play at once! A great HR professional is able to interpret the guidelines, consider the history of informal practices and unique circumstances of the issues, and deliver a path to the solution that is compliant and conforms with best practices.

Dual Perspective

In human resources, we represent both the needs of the employer and the needs of the employee. This is a challenging balance because often, you will recognize merit and shortcomings on both sides. A successful HR practitioner can work with all stakeholders to develop relationships and shared understandings around an issue, and furthermore guide the interactions in search of resolution.

Empathy

No matter the situation or its circumstances, one must show compassion to those involved, for their privacy and the right to be treated fairly and objectively. Whether you are terminating an employee or investigating them for an alleged policy violation, an HR HERO approaches people consistently in the workplace. Alternatively, you may support employees through difficult situations where a listening ear is needed no matter what time of day it happens to be.

Don't miss out!

Click the button below and you can sign up to receive emails whenever Rachel Hays publishes a new book. There's no charge and no obligation.

Sign Me Up!

https://books2read.com/r/B-A-TMKD-XRWK

BOOKS 2 READ

Connecting independent readers to independent writers.

64843291R00028

Made in the USA
Lexington, KY
21 June 2017